a smart girl's guide

Babysitting

the care and keeping of kids

by Harriet Brown
illustrations by Karen Wolcott

Published by American Girl Publishing
Copyright © 1999, 2007, 2014 American Girl

Questions or comments? Call 1-800-845-0005,
visit **americangirl.com,** or write to Customer Service,
American Girl, 8400 Fairway Place,
Middleton, WI 53562-0497.

Printed in China
14 15 16 17 18 19 20 LEO 10 9 8 7 6 5 4 3 2

Editorial Development: Trula Magruder
Art Direction: Lisa Wilber
Production: Judith Lary, Paula Moon, Kendra Schluter, Jeannette Bailey

A special thanks to Molly Kelly, American Red Cross, Badger Chapter

An important note to girls and parents:

What should you do when a child won't stop crying? How can you win over a shy six-year-old? What are the best games to play with babies? How do you handle a tantrum that goes on . . . and on . . . and on? This book has the answers to these questions and many more—including tips and tricks from experienced sitters.

But reading this book will **not** make you a certified baby-sitter. Books can't take the place of hands-on training—and books can't teach you everything you need to know about first aid and CPR.

Take this book to the job. The chapter on first aid will remind you what to do in an emergency—but it will not replace a first-aid class. To be certified, you must take a babysitter training course, such as the one offered by the American Red Cross.

You need knowledge to care for children. So before bounding into the babysitting business, find out about babysitter training in your town, and sign up. Taking a course and reading books like this one will get you started. Before long, you'll have the confidence to tell your clients, "I am the best babysitter—ever!"

Your friends at American Girl

contents

ready?

babysitter basics

Whether you're a new sitter or an old pro, see if these questions challenge your nanny knowledge!

1. To be a parent's helper, you don't need to . . .
    a. entertain children.
    b. keep children safe while they play.
    c. care for children when their parents go out.
    d. change diapers.

2. Your first babysitting job won't be easier just because you . . .
    a. turned 12 years old.
    b. worked as a parent's helper.
    c. took a Red Cross babysitting course.
    d. helped care for your younger siblings.

3. To get a babysitting job, you should never . . .
   a. hand out flyers to your parents' friends.
   b. accept a job from someone who just moved in down the street.
   c. work for your parents for free to gain experience.
   d. inform families that you've worked for as a parent's helper that you're ready to babysit.

4. The worst way to find out what you should charge for your first babysitting job is to . . .
   a. ask friends who babysit what they charge.
   b. ask neighbors what they pay.
   c. wait to see what the clients pay you, and then you'll know.
   d. ask your parents what they pay.

5. You should never cancel a babysitting job because . . .

  a. you're feeling sick.
  b. a family emergency came up at the last minute.
  c. your friend called you the day before with ice show tickets.
  d. your parents don't know the clients and asked you to cancel.

6. If your babysitting job isn't in your neighborhood, the best way to get to work and back is to . . .

  a. tell your client you'll need transportation.
  b. walk.
  c. take a bus.
  d. ask a neighbor to drive you to the job.

7. It's OK to turn down a babysitting job if . . .

  a. the children are terrors.
  b. the client has infant twins, and you don't think you can handle them.
  c. you feel uncomfortable in the home.
  d. all of the above.

8. When you're on the job, it's important to call the client right away if . . .

   a. the family runs out of peanut butter, and that's the only thing the child says she will eat.

   b. you called 911 because the baby's temperature jumped to 104 degrees.

   c. you don't know how to use the fancy TV remote, so the toddler's throwing a temper tantrum.

   d. all of the above.

9. If a client tells you to make yourself at home, you should feel free to . . .

   a. peek inside her closet and check out her shoe collection.
   b. invite your friends to come over and watch a movie.
   c. text your best friend about your day at school on the phone the client gave you.
   d. none of the above.

10. Be sure to call 911 if . . .

   a. the child falls from a high spot, such as a dresser, but seems fine.
   b. the child has a cut that won't stop bleeding.
   c. the child choked on piece of candy, but you used the Heimlich maneuver to remove it, and now she's OK.
   d. all of the above.

answers

1. c: As a parent's helper, you'll be responsible for taking care of kids while the parents are at home. For instance, you might be inside with a child while her parent works in the garden. Then if a problem comes up, you can ask that parent for help. Many sitters start out as parents' helpers because it's great practice.

2. a: Age has little to do with understanding how to handle children. Some girls don't feel ready to babysit until they're 14. Others feel ready at 11. The Red Cross recommends that babysitters start at age 11 but practice as a parent's helper until then.

3. b: If the family is new to the block, it's likely your parents don't know them yet. Before you take any job, discuss it with your parents. Make sure they know the family you'll be babysitting for. If you do get a job, remember to write down the time the job starts and the address, even if you think you'll remember.

4. c: Don't wait to see what a client will pay you. It's best for you and your client if you set a fair price and tell your customer what you charge before you take the job. Most girls charge $4 to $10 per hour based on where the customer lives and the number and ages of the kids they're sitting. Some babysitters charge a flat fee for the evening.

answers, continued

5. c: How would you feel if you were set to do something fun and someone said you couldn't? That's how parents feel when you cancel. If an ice show or anything else fun pops up the day before a job, swallow hard and tell your friend that you've made other plans.

6. a: Transportation to and from the job is usually part of the deal when it's out of the neighborhood—especially if you let the clients know ahead of time that you'll need a lift. But use your judgment. If for any reason at all you're nervous about someone taking you home, call your parents to come and get you.

7. d: You don't have to accept every job you're offered. Say something like, "I don't think we're a good fit," or "I won't be available, but thanks for thinking of me."

8. b: Any time you call 911, call the parents immediately after you call for help. But if a child won't stop crying, stay calm. Keep a cool head so that you can do what you're trained to do. Never call with a complaint, but remember: it is OK to call your parents or the child's parents for help if you really need it.

9. d: You should feel relaxed enough to take care of the children and yourself. If you're hungry, get a snack. But don't make a mess, tie up the phone, or secretly invite friends over. And never snoop! How would you feel if someone poked around in your room while you were out? Respect your client's privacy.

10. d: If a baby falls from a high height and seems fine, call 911. She may have internal injuries that you can't see. If you can't stop the child's bleeding from a deep cut, call 911. Even if you dislodge an object from a choking child, call 911 to make sure she is in good health. Though serious accidents rarely occur, if they do happen while you're on the job, the clients will expect you to call 911.

how did you score?

0–3 points
helping hands

Babysitting isn't for you—yet! Read this book to get a better idea of what it takes to care for kids. Then start helping out with your younger siblings, cousins, or neighbors' children. Eventually, you'll be ready to sit solo.

4–6 points
budding babysitter

You might not be ready for infant twins, but you are wise enough to understand that it's your responsibility to know all you can. After all, no one wants to make mistakes when caring for children. If you're already a mother's helper, add to your skills. Check out a Red Cross babysitting course or other child-care class offered in your community.

7–10 points
natural nanny

You've got what it takes to make a smart sitter. Read this book to fill in any information gaps you may have about caring for children. Take a safety class. Then get experience. Knowledge can build your confidence, and practice can build your skills. Before long, you'll be known as the best sitter on your block!

what do I need to know before the parents leave?

Ask the parents **anything** you're not sure about. The first time you babysit for a family, arrive a few minutes early and get the facts you need. Here are just a few ideas for what to ask.

What's this address and phone number in case I need to let someone know?

What's your cell-phone number so I can reach you in an emergency?

What time do you expect to be home?

Can you give me the name and number of the children's doctor and hospital?

May I have the name and phone number of a neighbor in case I need help immediately?

Do the children have any allergies to foods or medicine?

Are any foods off-limits?

What time should the kids go to bed?

Are the children taking any medications I need to know about?

Are there any snacks I can and can't eat?

What and when do you want me to feed the children?

Do you have a preferred way to discipline the children? For example, time-outs or no TV?

What should I do with the dirty diapers and clothes?

What's the poison control center's number?

If I have to call 911 for anything, I'll call you immediately after, if that's OK.

Are there any bedtime rituals for each child?

What's the name of the nearest intersection to this house in case I need to call 911?

15

super sitter secret

A big plus

"I took a Red Cross babysitting course in my town. I recommend it for girls who want to be good babysitters. Plus, parents will be more apt to trust you with their kids if they know you're certified!"

Emily

Oregon

don't
go!

everything's OK

You've arrived on time and met the child. You've gotten the list of last-minute instructions. Then Mom and Dad wave good-bye and close the door behind them—and the child bursts into tears. Now what?

Take a deep breath. These tears have nothing to do with you. It's normal for kids—especially little ones five and under—to get upset when their parents leave. These feelings even have a name: separation anxiety. With your help, most kids will cheer up pretty quickly once their parents are gone. Here's what you should do.

Reassure them.

Remind the child that his parents will be back in a little while. Even though he knows this, he may feel for a minute or two as if

his parents will be gone forever!

Saying the following words will help more than you think:

"Don't worry. Mom and Dad will be home later."

Connect with them.

You can also hold his hands and clap them together while you sing the words as a silly song:

"Mommy goes away and Mommy comes back."

It may sound corny to you, but it really does help. You want kids to trust you, so always tell the truth about when their parents will return. Never promise a toddler that her parents will be back at bedtime if you don't expect them home until much later. If you know her parents will be home late, you could say something like, "When you wake up tomorrow morning, Mom and Dad will be right here at home."

Then distract them.

Some babysitters bring little treats for just this moment—a stick of gum for an older child, a colorful adhesive-bandage strip for a toddler. Other babysitters plan a special activity. These treats and games don't have to be fancy. They just have to help kids get over the hump of saying good-bye.

Offer a hug.

Settle the child onto your lap with a favorite story.

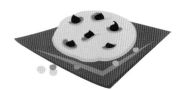

Put on music and dance around together.

Offer a small treat, such as a cookie.

Ask the child to show you her room.

Ask to see her toys.

Pull out a clean sock or pot
holder to use as a puppet.

Ask about her pets.

Pull out a pack of crayons
and color a picture.

Put on a DVD.

If it's OK with the parents,
take the child for a walk.

Say, "Whatever you do,
don't smile!"

What do you do when the crying won't stop?

You've tried every distraction you can think of and the child is still crying. **Take a deep breath and stay calm.** If a child is crying because her parents have just left, say something like, "Your mommy loves you very much. She and your dad are going to the movies. I know they'll miss you." **It doesn't matter *what* you say—what you're really telling the child is that it's OK to feel sad for a while.** She'll let you know when she's ready for fun.

But what if the crying *never* stops?

If you've checked the child's diaper and tried to feed and soothe her, but the crying continues, then it's time to get help. Babies and toddlers can't tell you what's wrong. They can't tell you if they're sick or in pain. So **before you break into tears yourself,** call your parents or the child's parents. They'll want to know what's going on. No one will get angry.

Big important point:

Sometimes asking for help
is the only thing you can do.

I'm hungry.

mealtime dos

Whether serving a snack or dinner, follow these basic rules to make mealtime a safe time.

Do make sure kids are safely occupied while you're preparing the meal.

Do check the temperature of the formula or milk. Shake a drop or two onto your wrist. If it feels hot to you, it's too hot for the baby.

Do have kids sit down at the table to eat.

Do feed kids only what parents have said is OK.

Do cut food into small pieces. Round-shaped foods, such as hot dogs and grapes, should be cut into half circles so that kids won't choke on them.

and don'ts

Don't serve food that is too hot to eat. Make sure it has cooled off before you put it on the table.

Don't leave leftovers out. Put them away in the fridge.

Don't walk away from a child who is eating—especially a baby. She can wriggle out of her chair and fall.

Don't serve drinks in fragile glasses. Use unbreakable cups instead.

Don't leave dirty dishes on the table. Rinse them and stack them in the sink.

fun food

Children can be picky eaters—remember when you wouldn't eat anything round or green? Your job is to serve them healthy snacks, not to fill them up with junk food. The key to feeding kids healthy food and keeping them happy is to make mealtime fun. Sound impossible? Try these tasty treats!

Bagel face

Spread cream cheese over half a bagel. Use vegetable or fruit pieces to make hair, eyes, and a smile.

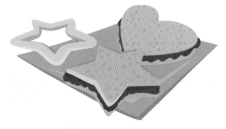

Cinnamon-sugar toast

Butter a slice of toast. Sprinkle a mixture of cinnamon and sugar over it. Cut off the crusts.

Sandwich shapes

Use cookie cutters to turn plain PB&J into hearts, stars, and other darling designs.

Cracker sandwiches

Make cracker sandwiches with peanut butter, jelly, cream cheese, tuna salad, or sliced turkey.

Peewee pizza

Spread tomato sauce onto an English muffin. Add cubes of cheese. Microwave on high until the cheese melts. Let the child make a face with cut vegetables.

Ants on a log

Spread peanut butter on a celery stick. Add a line of raisins.

silly servings

Sometimes *what* you feed kids isn't as important as *how* you feed them. A giggle or two can make everything taste better!

Switcheroo

Let kids pretend they're the babysitters and you're the kid. Ask them to serve you—and themselves—a premade snack.

Restaurant

Pretend the kids have come to a restaurant. You're the server (and cook!). Tell them "today's special." Write their orders on a notepad. While you're preparing the meal, give them paper and crayons. Let them know that they have to "pay" for the meal with artwork!

Indoor picnic

Spread a tablecloth or old sheet on the floor. Pack simple picnic food in lunch boxes or in a picnic basket. Pour juice or milk from a thermos.

super sitter secret

Smooth sailing

"I like to make happy faces on sandwiches with raisins for the eyes and mouth. Or I stick a straw in the sandwich and tape on a paper sail for a sandwich boat!"

Robin
Vermont

cleanup time!

If there's one thing parents dislike, it's coming home to a messy kitchen. So make sure that you **clean up after yourself** and the children. You don't have to wash every dish, but tidy up the kitchen the best you can. If you're caring for an infant, you won't have time to clean. That's OK. Even grown-ups let chores slide when they're taking care of a baby!

Most kids enjoy helping with cleanup. Make up a silly song, such as "Clean up, clean up, everybody clean up!" or "Kristy is a helper, a helper, a helper. Kristy is a helper, yes she is." Choose chores that are right for each age. Toddlers and preschoolers can dry silverware and put it away. School-age kids can load the dishwasher or wash dishes. If you're not sure where something goes, ask. **Kids love knowing more than you do!**

your turn

I'm hungry!

You forgot to eat before you came to babysit, and now you're starving. What should you do?

No one wants you to go hungry. Help yourself to a snack: cheese and crackers, a peanut butter sandwich, cookies and milk. But don't open foil-wrapped packages or dig through the freezer. Parents won't appreciate it if you eat tomorrow night's dinner!

wanna play?

baby play

Want to be everyone's favorite babysitter? Just remember these three little words: play with kids. What kids want most is your attention. Chances are, the kids you're babysitting will love anything you suggest, as long as you do it together.

Little ones need simple games. Be prepared to play them over and over!

Where's the ball?

Sit opposite baby on the floor. Gently roll a ball toward her. Say something like, "Where's the ball? There it is! Can you roll it back to me?"

Which hand?

Put a toy in one hand. Put both hands behind your back and ask baby to point to the hand that has the toy.

super sitter secret

Dress the part

"Don't wear necklaces or dangling earrings. Babies love to pull on them, and you could end up with sore ears or a broken necklace. Wear nice but comfortable clothes. You'll look professional and still be able to crawl around with the kids."

Melissa
Indiana

Want to sing?

Don't forget all those songs you learned as a child. Try singing "Itsy-Bitsy Spider," "I'm a Little Teapot," and "Head, Shoulders, Knees, and Toes." And remember: it's all new to them!

See the animal?

Place stuffed animals throughout the house. Now walk baby through the house, pointing out and naming every animal you see: "Look, there's a bunny! I see a penguin. Do you see the kitty cat?"

Dance with me!

Put on some music and get moving! Babies love it when you spin them around. But don't do it right after a meal, and stop if you get dizzy.

Look what I see!

Carry baby around the room, pointing out interesting objects—a vase of flowers, a ticking clock. Let her look out the window, and talk to her about what's outside: "Look, there's a tree with colorful leaves."

toddler time

Toddlers think everything's funny. The best games and activities for them are short and silly!

Color clues

Toddlers love to be right—especially when you're wrong! Sing, "Timmy is a big boy, a big boy, a big boy. Timmy is a big boy, and his shirt is green!" Be sure to say the wrong color. The first few times you might have to correct yourself: "Green? Noooooo, it's purple!" Soon *he'll* be correcting you!

Planet Purr

Pretend the sofa is a spaceship. With the child in your lap, lean left and right as the ship zooms into space. Once you "land," climb off onto Planet Purr, where everyone becomes a kitty! Get onto the ship to become human again.

Peewee pet care

For this game, you'll need a toy truck or car, strips of cloth, and a few stuffed animals. Ask the toddler to bandage the "injured" animals and transport them in the ambulance. Don't forget the siren!

Change machine

Drape a sheet over a table. Every time a child goes through the "change machine," she becomes something new—a firefighter, frisky puppy, or ballerina!

Around town

Turn cardboard boxes into a town. Get out toy cars and as many doll townspeople as you can find.

Creative coloring

Make a one-of-a-kind coloring book. Fold three sheets of construction paper in half. Staple them together to make a book. Draw pictures of the child, her parents, and her pets. Ask her to color them in.

kid games

Older kids have their own ideas about how to have fun. Offer these games when they're ready for something new.

Basketball

Crumple pieces of newspaper to make ten balls for each kid. Set out a waste basket. Each child tries to make as many baskets as possible.

Magazine scavenger hunt

Give each child an old magazine or catalogue, along with a list of things to find, cut out, and glue onto paper.

Card games

Bring a deck of cards, and show kids a new game each time you babysit. In Concentration, lay out all the cards facedown. Take turns flipping over two cards. If the numbers match, pick up the cards and take another turn. At the end, the player with the most cards wins!

Letter writing

Ask kids to "send" you letters, describing what they want to do the next time you babysit. Let them seal the letters in envelopes and drop them into a "mailbox" or "mailbag" you've set out. Read them when you get home.

Soft volleyball

Lay a piece of string across the floor, and have kids stand on either side. Blow up a balloon. Toss it back and forth without letting it touch the ground.

Junior babysitter

Older kids love coming up with games for the little ones. Put them in charge of creating activities for toddlers or babies. Be sure to play the games with them!

super sitter secret

Clean queen

"One time I was babysitting four little girls. They were bored, and the house was a mess. So I invented a game. In each room, a girl was the queen and the rest of us were servants. She told us what to pick up or clean. We appointed a new queen for each room. It worked like a charm, and their mom was happy about the house!"

Anna
Washington

pack up!

Kids will get a kick out of anything you bring along. Your goodies don't have to be new—they'll be new to the kids, and that's all that matters.

- Children's DVDs or music CDs
- Colorful adhesive-bandage strips
- Toys (but not tiny toys; try trucks, dolls, etc.)
- Stuffed animals
- Puppets (can be made from socks or oven mitts)
- Bubbles

- Stickers
- Board games
- Playing cards
- Children's books
- Old catalogs or magazines
- Paper and envelopes
- Coloring books and crayons

she
hit me!

cool them off

Uh-oh. The kids have been arguing—and arguing—all evening. You feel more like a referee than a babysitter! How can you stop the squabbling?

First, make sure the kids don't hurt each other, and give everyone a little time to settle down. Put the children in different rooms or in opposite corners of the same room. Tell them, "We're all going to take a time-out for five minutes." Set a timer, and make sure everybody's quiet until it rings.

Sort it

Many arguments aren't about anything important—they're the way kids let off steam at one another. But when real conflicts do come up, it's your job to help sort things out.

Talk about it

The best way to do that is to have the kids talk to each other. Stand one on either side of you, facing each other. Give each child two minutes to express her feelings. A few important rules: The kids must talk to each other, not to you. They must talk about their own feelings, not just rehash what the other one said or did. And they must really listen to what the other child says.

Work on it

Once both kids have aired their feelings, the argument may be over. But if the kids are still fighting, you have to help them work it out. Ask each of them to offer a fair solution to the problem. If they can't come up with a plan they both like, offer a compromise. If the argument is over a doll, for instance, you might suggest that each child take a five-minute turn with the doll. Or point out another doll that could be added to the game.

Settle it

If the kids just can't agree, let them know that you will solve the problem your way—by taking away the toy or ending the game. Give them one more chance to work it out, and then do what you said you would.

super sitter secret

Funny face

"When kids are fighting, I set them on chairs across from each other and tell them to give each other ugly faces. Before you know it, they can't frown, and they end up laughing!"

Jen
Wisconsin

I'm telling!

Kids tell on each other for two reasons.

They can't solve the problem.

Help kids talk to each other to try to resolve the problem themselves. If they can't, *you* make a decision—and make sure everyone sticks to it.

They want your attention.

Play with the kids. If they don't want you to play, stay close enough to hear what's going on. Let them know you're around. They'll be glad, even if they don't seem to care. If they're still tattling, say, "I won't listen to tattling, but I *will* listen if you want to tell me how *you* feel or about something *you* did."

A happy medium

"While I was babysitting, one kid wanted to watch one movie and the other wanted to watch a different movie. I asked them to decide on their own, and I went to fix popcorn. When I came back, the kids had agreed to the first movie because they had seen the other one before."

Carly

Wisconsin

I'm scared.

little kids

Babies and toddlers can't say "I'm scared" in words. Instead, they tell you with tears. To comfort little ones who are frightened or upset, try the following ideas.

Talk

Babies may not understand *what* you say, but they react to the way you say it. Talk to them in a low, soothing voice, and keep talking even if you run out of things to say. For instance: "There, there, baby, everything's OK, you're OK, everyone loves you, you're going to be fine, you'll see, it's OK."

Walk

Movement helps calm kids. Pick up a baby or toddler and walk her around the room or house.

Touch

Start with a hug. Move on to patting or rubbing the baby's back, bottom, or chest. Find a steady rhythm she likes, and rub or pat firmly (but not hard enough to hurt).

Distract

Once the baby starts to calm down, distract her with a toy, a book, a peek out the window, or anything else that catches her interest.

Use body language

Long before they learn to talk, children communicate with body language. You can use this special language to comfort kids. Kneel beside the child so that you can look into her eyes. Smile. Tilt your head to one side. After you do this a few times, it will feel natural. Try it—it works!

super sitter secret

Travel light

"I *always* bring a night-light in my backpack when I go babysitting. Some kids are very afraid of the dark!"

Joan
Rhode Island

45

three and up

Kids this age can usually tell you exactly what's scaring them. That helps! Once you know what's frightening them, you can do something about it. Here are some of the most common fears children have.

The dark

Don't flip off the lights and race to a lit room yourself. This can make kids nervous about the dark. Dim the lights or put on a night-light. Then let them see that you're not afraid. Sit on the bed and tell them a story. Or give them a favorite stuffed animal or doll. Say, "Put your baby to sleep." This puts them in charge of their fear.

Stormy weather

You'll find out about this fear only if a thunderstorm actually happens while you're babysitting. Stay with the child. Turn on a light even if she has already gone to bed. Talk to her about what a thunderstorm really is, in words she can understand: "Thunder is the noise we hear when two big rain clouds bump into each other up in the sky. Isn't that cool?" Hug her, play with her, sing songs, tell funny stories, or do anything else that takes her mind off the storm outside.

Scary thoughts or dreams

Tell the child to imagine that her mind is a television and she's holding the remote control. Have her imagine that she's clicking the remote and changing the channel from a scary show to a silly one. Sit with her until she's asleep.

your turn

Night noises

You just finished watching a scary movie on TV, and now you hear strange noises in the house. What do you do when *you're* scared?

The best cure for this kind of fear is prevention. Don't watch scary movies or read scary books —especially while you're babysitting. If you do get nervous, check the house to reassure yourself that everything's secure. Call a parent or a neighbor. If you're truly convinced you hear an intruder, call 911. It's better to be safe than sorry.

Mash the monsters!

No matter how often you reassure them, some kids will still be afraid of things that go bump in the night. If this happens, get creative. Here's what other sitters have done to move the monsters out.

"I bring a spray bottle filled with water. At bedtime, I tell the kids it's monster spray and spray it around the room. Then I tuck it back into my pack, and they feel safe!"
Channing
Kansas

"If the kids say there's a monster under their bed, I put a carrot into a sack and slip it under the bed. I tell them monsters love carrots, and they shrink to fit inside the bag. After a few minutes, I grab the bag and put it into the garbage can. They always fall asleep right after that!"
Kelly
California

"The four-year-old that I watch is afraid of the dark. So we surround the bed with his stuffed animals. We call them Super Toys. They keep out bogeymen and ghosts."
Laura
Maryland

but my mom lets me!

you're in charge

The kids you're babysitting insist that they always have candy with dinner. You know that's not true—but what do you do?

Kids can be surprisingly persuasive when they want you to do things their way. Try these wise words the next time you don't know what to say.

Offer a substitute

He says: "My parents make me hot chocolate every night—and they let me drink it in bed."

You say: "Hot chocolate in bed doesn't seem like a good idea to me. I'll give you a glass of milk and read you a story while you drink it in the kitchen."

Offer a substitute that you feel good about. Ask parents about the rules when they get home so that next time you'll know.

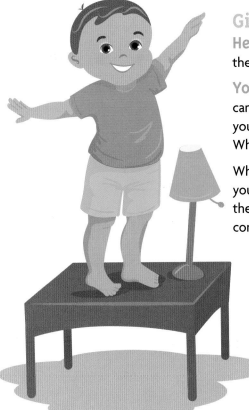

Give him a choice

He says: "I just want to jump off the table *one* time."

You say: "You have a choice. You can either climb down from the table yourself, or I can help you down. Which do you choose?"

When you give children a choice, you're teaching them that you make the rules but that they have some control over what happens.

Think about safety

She says: "Don't tell my parents! I'll never ride my bike without my helmet again, I promise!"

You say: "I do have to tell your parents—not to be mean, but because I know they care about you. When it comes to your safety, they have to know exactly what happened."

When the parents return, let them know what the child has done. Remember: your job is to keep kids safe, even if it makes you unpopular.

Enforce the rules—calmly

She says: "I won't get ready for bed! I hate you! I wish you would go away and never come back!"

You say (calmly): "I'm sorry you feel that way. But you still have to brush your teeth."

Sometimes kids say mean things to see how you'll react, but they'll usually calm down and do what you ask. If you feel a child really doesn't like you, let her parents know. Say, "I'm sorry, but Ellie and I aren't a good fit." They'll understand.

51

Make an agreement

He says: "I'm not cleaning up my toys, and you can't make me!"

You say: "I can't make you, and I'm not going to try. But if you don't clean up, I won't have time to read you a story, because I'll be too busy cleaning up toys. And I will have to tell your parents what happened."

Show the child that his behavior has consequences. And if you do decide to take away a story or a treat, don't back down.

Stay calm

He says: "I'm not going to bed! No, no, no, no, no!"

You say: Nothing. You don't want to keep the tantrum going. Stay near him, but let him cry. He will eventually calm down.

Sometimes silence works best. Kids try tantrums to see if they'll get what they want. If tantrums work, they'll keep throwing them—which is not good for anybody.

super sitter secret

You're the boss

"Even though you may not feel like it, you are in charge. The kids look up to you!"

Heather
Connecticut

poop.

get ready!

Never changed a diaper? It's easier than you think. But before you face your first diaper duty, ask an adult to show you how. Then remember these tips.

Stock supplies

Once the baby's on the table, you must not leave her, so get supplies ready *before* you lay her down: baby wipes, clean diapers, and any cream or ointment the parents have asked you to apply. Keep supplies out of the way so that the baby can't kick them off. Also, place a garbage can or diaper pail nearby to dispose of used diapers.

Never leave her

If you can, keep one hand on the baby so that she doesn't fall off the table—and *never* leave her side.

Distract her

Babies love to watch things that move. If there's a mobile over the changing area, blow on it or tap it right before you get to work. You can also talk, sing, or make faces at the baby.

Keep her busy

Give the baby something to hold or chew during a diaper change so that her hands don't get in your way. If no toys are handy, offer a clean diaper or washcloth.

Be gentle

To avoid bumping the baby's head, keep one hand under the back of her head as you lay her down.

Remove her clothes

When removing the baby's pants, keep a hand on her. If her clothes are dirty, put clean ones on after you've changed the diaper.

diaper demo

Once everything's prepared, you're ready to change the diaper. If the family doesn't use a slip-on diaper, follow these step-by-step instructions.

1. Undo diaper. Gently grasp baby's ankles and lift. Slide diaper from under baby's bottom. Fold edges so that nothing falls out.

2. Set baby's bottom down gently. Dispose of used diaper, but keep a hand on baby at all times. Even a newborn can roll off a changing table.

3. Carefully wipe baby's bottom from front to back with a baby wipe. For boys, lay a clean diaper over the penis to avoid surprising showers.

4. Apply lotion if parents have asked you to. Then gently grasp baby's feet and lift. Slide a clean diaper under baby's bottom, and fasten the tabs from back to front.

5. Dress the baby in clean clothes if necessary. Then set her someplace safe—in a crib or on the carpet where you can see her—while you wash your hands.

potty plan

Most kids begin toilet training between ages two and three. And every child goes through the process differently. To help kids do their best, try these tips:

- When a child says she has to go potty, she means right now! So don't say, "Wait a minute." Stop what you're doing, and take her to the bathroom.

- Never scold a child who wets his pants. If he doesn't make it to the toilet, praise him for trying, and help him into clean clothes. When he does go potty on the toilet, always praise him.

- Boys may sit down to pee—it's neater that way. If they want to stand, help aim their bodies so that they're peeing into the toilet.

- Kids under five may need help cleaning up after pooping. Ask the child to stand and lean over. This makes your job easier. Remember to wipe front to back.

- Two- and three-year-olds often forget to go to the bathroom. Every so often, ask the the child, "Do you need to go potty?" But don't force the issue.

- Make sure the child washes before she leaves the bathroom. Squirt soap into her hands and turn on warm water. Remember to wash your hands, too, especially after changing diapers.

ow!

safety first

Stop accidents before they happen.

Check for potential hazards

Watch out for possible dangers, such as matches, electrical cords, plastic bags, cleaners, medicines, tools, and even clutter. Use childproof locks and childproof socket covers if they're available, and keep bathroom doors closed.

Never tell a stranger that you're alone.

Make sure the child can't pull anything off a high area onto herself.

Never leave out knives.

Keep rugs flat so that kids won't trip over them.

Don't leave the house

As soon as parents leave, lock all doors. If someone knocks on a door, don't open it. Say, "Mr. Smith can't come to the door, but he asked me to take a message." If someone calls, don't tell the caller you're alone. Say, "I'm sorry, Ms. Smith isn't available right now. Can I take a message?"

Know your job site

Ask parents where they keep the first-aid kit, flashlight, and fire extinguisher. Ask how to work the alarm system, the smoke detector, and any equipment you'll be allowed to use, such as the DVD player, TV, or microwave.

Know where the emergency equipment is kept.

FIRST AID

Keep plants out of reach.

Keep all cabinets shut.

Face pot handles toward the back of the stove.

Always keep an eye on children

In the blink of an eye, babies can stuff tiny objects into their mouths. Toddlers can slip into pools, tubs, or toilets. Older kids can disappear around a corner. So keep your eyes on kids at all times. Continue to check on them even after they go to bed.

be prepared

Emergencies are less scary when you know what to do. Being prepared will help you to **stay calm.** Take the Babysitter's Training Course offered by the American Red Cross, or Safe Sitter classes held at a hospital in your community.

No matter how minor a child's injury—from a bee sting to a nose-bleed—**call the parents.** That doesn't mean always call the parents immediately. In some cases, you'll need to call 911 or the poison control center, or help the child yourself, before you call anyone. Once the child has been helped, then inform the parents.

When working around blood, **always wear rubber gloves.** First-aid kits should have gloves, but buy a pair and keep them in your baby-sitter's bag just in case. If you don't have gloves with you, scrub your hands with soap and water afterwards.

This is not a first-aid book. **Nothing replaces hands-on first-aid training.** But the following basic tips will help guide you through emergencies.

Insect stings and bites

If you see a stinger, scrape it off with something stiff, like a stiff plastic or playing card. Wash bites and stings with soap and water. Wrap an ice cube in a paper towel and hold it to a sting to reduce swelling.

Cuts and scrapes

Small cuts and scrapes can bleed quite a bit. Use a clean washcloth to press lightly on the injury until the bleeding stops. Then gently wash the cut with soap and water. Apply an adhesive-bandage strip—even if you don't think one is needed. It will make the child feel better.

Nosebleeds

Tilt the child's head forward. Pinch the bottom of the nose closed to stop the bleeding. Never tilt the head backward.

Fever

If a child feels warmer than usual to the touch, call the parents. In the meantime, encourage the child to rest and offer her water or juice to drink.

Heavy bleeding

For a wound that spurts or gushes, **call 911 immediately.** If someone else is in the area, ask that person to call 911. Then press a clean cloth firmly against the wound, and position the body so that the wound is raised higher than the heart. Keep pressing for at least five minutes. When the bleeding stops, tape the cloth in place and keep the child warm until help arrives.

super sitter secret

Seeing red

"If kids get a small cut, use a red or dark-colored towel so that the blood doesn't scare them."

Sarah
Wisconsin

choking

If a choking child can't talk, cough, or breathe, you must get rid of the obstruction immediately. *Don't take the time to call 911 unless the child passes out.* (If someone else can call 911 for you, ask him or her to do so.) **As soon as you've forced the object out, call 911.** Choking is *very* scary. Even after you've taken a first-aid course, continue to practice these steps on a doll so that you'll be prepared.

For a child:

1. Give 5 back blows.
Bend the child at the waist and give 5 back blows between the shoulder blades with the heel of one hand.

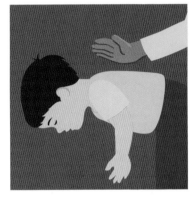

2. Give 5 belly thrusts.
Stand behind the child. Wrap your arms around his waist. Place a fist with the thumb side against his stomach, just above the belly button. Grab the fist with your other hand. Give 5 quick, upward belly thrusts.

3. Repeat if needed.
Repeat with 5 back blows and 5 belly thrusts until whatever the child is choking on pops out of his mouth and he starts to breathe.

For an infant:

1. Position the baby.

Sit down. Turn the infant onto his belly. Lay him facedown along your arm. Hold his jaw to support his head. Don't cover his nose or mouth. Keep his head lower than his body.

2. Give 5 back blows.

Use the heel of one hand to push the blows between the shoulder blades.

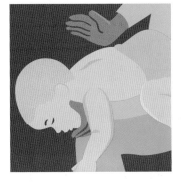

3. Place baby on back.

While supporting the head, turn the child over onto his back. Place three fingers in the center of the infant's chest just below the nipple line.

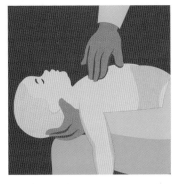

4. Do chest compressions.

Press down firmly on the chest five times. Repeat with 5 back blows and 5 chest compressions until the object comes out and the infant can breathe.

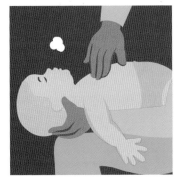

Minor burns

Run cool water over red, unbroken skin for at least five minutes. Cover the burn loosely with a clean (sterile) dressing. Don't put on an adhesive bandage strip. Don't apply medicine, butter, or any kind of cream. Don't use ice. Small burns are painful, so reassure the child that she'll be OK. Call the parents. For any burn worse than red skin or a small blister, cool with water and **call 911 immediately**—even if you aren't sure how bad the burn is. Then call the parents.

Swallowing nonfood

If a child swallows anything that isn't food, **call the poison control center immediately** at 1-800-222-1222. (If you can't remember the number, call 911.) Have whatever the child swallowed nearby or be prepared to describe what the child swallowed when you call. You may be asked to give the child milk or water to drink. Call the parents.

Call 911

If you're faced with any other emergency, **call 911.** The 911 operator may ask for the address and will want to know what kind of emergency is going on. Stay calm, and follow the operator's instructions.

I'm not tired!

make a timetable

How do you turn a bouncing child into a sleeping angel? Read on!

Putting children to bed takes time and planning. Allow 30 to 45 minutes for changing into pajamas, brushing teeth, reading books or telling a story, and cuddling. For instance, if the parents have asked you to put the kids to bed at 8:30, start getting them ready no later than 7:45. Babies and toddlers are a different story. Ask parents what routines they follow to get their tiny ones to sleep.

Calm down

Who would want to go to bed when it sounds like others are having a good time? So, an hour before bedtime, dim the lights. Turn down (or turn off) the TV or stereo. Put away noisy toys and computer games, and pull out books or engage kids in quiet activities, such as jigaw puzzles or solitaire. Signal to the child that things are slowing down.

Give plenty of warning

Kids need help moving from one activity to another. Saying, "It's bedtime right now!" is sure to cause tears and tantrums. Instead say, "In ten minutes we're going to get you ready for bed."

Follow routines

Kids often have bedtime routines. Ask parents about these. At what time do the kids get into their pajamas? Do they need to pick up their toys before bed? Can they have a snack? Should you leave the bedroom light on or turn it off?

Share a story

Stories are a great way to end the day. Slip kids into bed, tuck them in, and then read or tell them a story. If the kids want to read to you, let them.

Be firm

Stick to the routine, especially the first time you sit for a family. When it's time for lights-out, be firm. Kids will know that you mean what you say—and will be much more likely to listen!

Sleepy-time tips

Many children need help falling asleep, especially babies and toddlers. Here are some tried-and-true ways to help.

Infant ideas

Rock or carry an infant. Try different moves—such as fast, slow, or up-and-down jiggling—until you find one that works.

Lay a sleeping baby down slowly. Dropping him into the crib will jolt him awake. Note: Babies under age one should be put to sleep on their backs to reduce the risk of sudden infant death syndrome.

Give a massage. Firmly pat or rub the infant's back or her tummy. You can try a combination of patting and rubbing.

Babies love soothing sounds, which is why they often sleep in the car. If the parents have a white-noise device, use it. Or bring a CD of soothing sounds such as a waterfall or waves rolling in on the shore.

Toddler tricks

Give a toddler a cuddly toy, a favorite blanket, or a T-shirt that smells like her mom or dad.

Sing to a child once she's in bed. Lullabies are good, but almost any song will help a child settle down.

Put on a night-light. Or turn on a light in the hall or bathroom and adjust the door until it feels open enough for the child.

Promise to come back and check on the child in 10 or 15 minutes—and make sure that you do.

I'm tired!

The kids are asleep, and you're tired, too. Is it OK for you to take a nap on the couch?

Falling asleep on the job is unprofessional, and it could be dangerous. Until the parents return, your job is to be alert and in charge. (A good night's sleep the night before should help.) Splash cold water on your face, jog in place —do whatever you must to stay awake.

are you free tonight?

Quiz

babysitting styles

After a few babysitting jobs, take this quiz to discover your sitting style. Circle the letter next to the answer that describes you best.

1. Asking questions about the children is always a good way to show your interest in a babysitting job. The question you'd most like to ask is . . .

   a. "What makes your children feel the happiest?"

   b. "What kind of games and activities do your children like?"

   c. "Do your children have any allergies or behavior problems that I should know about?"

2. Two toddler brothers are fighting over a toy. You . . .
   a. sit down and show them how to share the toy. For example, if it's a ball, you roll it to one and then to the other.
   b. turn the fight into fun. For example, you take the toy, tell the boys that you have magical powers and can enlarge it, and then pretend you're the giant-sized version of the toy until they start giggling and forget about their disagreement.
   c. remove the toy and give each of them a different toy.

3. Three-year-old Samantha refuses to put on her coat for your walk in the backyard. You . . .
   a. say, "OK, but it's really cold." And you bring her coat to give to her when she says she's cold.
   b. ask, "Are you three?" When she nods, say, "Hmm, that means you need three layers for our magical trip." Then dress her in three layers that will keep her toasty.
   c. tell her that she has to wear a coat or she can't go outside. Then give her a choice of coats. She'll choose one.

4. Andy's parents asked you to give their son his medication, but every time you offer it to him, he turns his head away. You . . .
   a. tell him he can have a lollipop if he takes it.
   b. pretend to taste it, and act as if it's the most amazing thing you've ever tasted in your life. Don't give in until he asks for a taste.
   c. give him an icy treat. In the middle of his licking, ask him to take his medicine so that he can continue to eat his ice cream. His numb tongue will help dull the flavor.

5. You've run through Abigail's usual bedtime routine, but she's still as perky as puppy's ears. You . . .

   a. say, "I'll let you stay up for 15 more minutes if you pick out the story for me to read while you're in bed."

   b. tell her you also work as the sleep fairy and your enchanting songs make girls drowsy. Then sing a lullaby as you gently bounce on her bed.

   c. knew ahead of time this would be a problem, so you ran her around like crazy earlier in the afternoon, gave her a warm bath right before bed, and then told her a story, keeping her calm and relaxed, until ZZZZ.

super sitter secret

Sweet dreams

"When I'm babysitting a child who can't read, and I read a story at bedtime, I always end with 'and they went to sleep and lived happily ever after,' even though most books don't say that. It helps the child think about going to sleep as a nice thing instead of dreading it."

Julia
Delaware

6. The child you're sitting tends to misbehave. To handle this, you . . .

   a. praise him every time he does something nice.

   b. distract him by playing games, making up dances, and having fun.

   c. bring along a premade chart, and give him a star for every half hour he doesn't misbehave.

7. The power goes out in a thunderstorm, and Lilly starts to cry. You . . .

   a. comfort her. You hold the little girl, soothe her, tell her it'll be all right, and then sing her a song.

   b. distract her. You hold up the child's pointer finger and tell her it's magic. Tell her that each time she touches you with it, you become a different animal.

   c. inform her. You pull out the flashlight you carried with you to the job, and turn it on. Then tell the child exactly what happened.

8. The parents are home, but they offer no indication that they're going to pay you. You . . .

   a. decide to give them the benefit of the doubt, and figure they'll remember next time.

   b. joke about it: "Can you wash my pay before you hand it over? That way I can make a clean getaway."

   c. know it's a job, and so you say, "We said $5 an hour, right? So that'll be $20 for tonight."

Answers

Did you choose mostly a's?

sweet sitter

Your style of child care is so sweet that kids can't resist you! Many parents probably appreciate this approach, but if you tend to melt if a kid demands something, this tactic could end up causing problems for you. So be sweet, but be firm when you need to.

Did you choose mostly b's?

spicy sitter

You add zip and zest to your jobs—and kids love that. When you play games and use your imagination with children, they feel like participants in their own child care. The only time this might be an issue is if a child doesn't take you seriously when she needs to. If this happens, speak in a sincere (but not angry) tone, and patiently insist that the child listen.

Did you choose mostly c's?

salty sitter

Salty means experienced, and you tend to pull problem-solving ideas from your babysitting bag of tricks. You know that it's important for you and the children to be safe and comfortable. But you also like to plan for things that might cause problems before they happen. A smart sitter makes responsible choices for children—not just popular ones.

What's your
sitter secret?

Write to

Babysitting Editor
American Girl
8400 Fairway Place
Middleton, WI 53562

(Sorry, but photos can't be returned. All comments
and suggestions received by American Girl may be
used without compensation or acknowledgment.)

Here are some other American Girl books you might like:

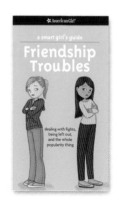